READING AND WRITING
JAPANESE KATAKANA

A Character Workbook for Beginners

EMIKO KONOMI

Illustrated by Jessica Anecito

TUTTLE Publishing

Tokyo | Rutland, Vermont | Singapore

"Books to Span the East and West"

Tuttle Publishing was founded in 1832 in the small New England town of Rutland, Vermont [USA]. Our core values remain as strong today as they were then—to publish best-in-class books which bring people together one page at a time. In 1948, we established a publishing office in Japan—and Tuttle is now a leader in publishing English-language books about the arts, languages and cultures of Asia. The world has become a much smaller place today and Asia's economic and cultural influence has grown. Yet the need for meaningful dialogue and information about this diverse region has never been greater. Over the past seven decades, Tuttle has published thousands of books on subjects ranging from martial arts and paper crafts to language learning and literature—and our talented authors, illustrators, designers and photographers have won many prestigious awards. We welcome you to explore the wealth of information available on Asia at **www.tuttlepublishing.com**.

Published by Tuttle Publishing, an imprint of Periplus Editions (HK) Ltd.

www.tuttlepublishing.com

Copyright © 2019 by Periplus Editions (HK) Ltd.

ISBN: 978-4-8053-1522-4

Distributed by:

North America, Latin America & Europe
Tuttle Publishing
364 Innovation Drive
North Clarendon, VT 05759-9436 U.S.A.
Tel: 1 (802) 773-8930
Fax: 1 (802) 773-6993
info@tuttlepublishing.com
www.tuttlepublishing.com

Asia Pacific
Berkeley Books Pte. Ltd.
3 Kallang Sector #04-01
Singapore 349278
Tel: (65) 6741-2178
Fax: (65) 6741-2179
inquiries@periplus.com.sg
www.tuttlepublishing.com

Japan
Tuttle Publishing
Yaekari Building, 3rd Floor
5-4-12 Osaki
Shinagawa-ku
Tokyo 141 0032
Tel: (81) 3 5437-0171
Fax: (81) 3 5437-0755
sales@tuttle.co.jp
www.tuttle.co.jp

First edition
25 24 23 22 21   6 5 4 3
Printed in Singapore   2111TP

TUTTLE PUBLISHING© is a registered trademark of Tuttle Publishing, a division of Periplus Editions (HK) Ltd.

CONTENTS

PART 1

Reading and Writing Katakana: The Basics

PART 2

Reading and Writing Katakana: Vocabulary Practice

To Download or Stream Online Audio and Printable Flashcards

1. You must have an internet connection.
2. Type the URL below into your web browser.
   https://www.tuttlepublishing.com/reading-and-writing-japanese-katakana2

For support, you can email us at info@tuttlepublishing.com.

How to Use This Book

Who is this book for?

The book is primarily designed for learners of Japanese who wish to master the reading and writing of *katakana*, one of the three fundamental scripts of the Japanese language, the others being *hiragana* and *kanji* (see page 7). The book is aimed at beginning-level students and no knowledge of Japanese grammar is required. However, new katakana words are coming into existence at an accelerating pace, and they can be surprisingly challenging at times, even for advanced level learners. Therefore, any Japanese learner will find this book useful and will benefit greatly by studying it.

When Japanese children are first learning to read and write, they learn the hiragana script before the katakana script. This book is designed so that it can be used without any knowledge of hiragana. However, I recommend learning hiragana first, using this book's companion title *Reading and Writing Japanese Hiragana*.

What is the purpose of this book?

The purpose of this book is to introduce the symbols of the katakana script and to provide ample practice material to promote practical competence in reading and writing.

Katakana symbols are introduced using plentiful sample words and expressions chosen for their common practical usage in contemporary Japan. They are selected for their utility in discussing subjects relevant to modern adult Japanese speakers. Learners will have abundant opportunity to practice through realistic drills and exercises.

How is this book structured?

This book is comprised of two chapters. The first chapter introduces the stroke order of each katakana symbol, along with basic reading and writing practice. The second chapter presents common and practical katakana vocabulary grouped into subject categories. Ample practice material is provided for each category. Drills and exercises are organized in a manner that ensures systematic progress. Online audio files recorded by native Japanese speakers are available on the Tuttle website (see address on page 6). These audio files are an excellent tool for learning the "sound-to-symbol" connection, and for hearing new vocabulary words being used in an authentic context.

How is katakana presented in this book?

Each symbol is first separately introduced following the traditional Japanese order. Grid-like boxes are provided to help learners write symbols with the correct stroke order, relative positioning and uniform size. Once learners are comfortable writing an individual symbol, they progress to practice writing that symbol within frequently used words that include it, rather than practice writing in isolation. The goal of reading and writing Japanese is not to merely recognize and write individual symbols, but rather to understand authentic texts. This book is designed to help learners achieve this goal.

Study tips

- Progress in order: each section is built upon preceding sections. Do not skip around.
- Practice mindfully: avoid mindless copying or tracing. Test your memory.
- Cover the model examples and see if you can reproduce the symbols on your own.
- Download free flashcards from this book's website at the link below to help you memorize the symbols.
- Once you have mastered the symbols, practice them in meaningful units of vocabulary rather than in isolation.
- Do the Reading and Writing Practice exercises in Part 2 in order: each exercise is built on preceding exercises.
- Download gridded writing sheets from this book's website at the address below for further handwriting practice.
- Use the online audio files at the address below for sound-symbol connection.
- Frequently revisit old material ("loop back").

Repetition is key in learning a language. It improves memory and fluency, builds up confidence, and helps with application. Set a learning schedule and stick to it to form good habits. Frequently revisit previously studied material. I suggest that after studying three new symbols, you loop back to the first two before moving on to the fourth. Once you are comfortable with five individual symbols, move beyond isolated symbols and practice reading them in meaningful words as soon as possible. You can choose your own pace at which to work, but make sure you loop back frequently.

Ideally, users of this book will have already learned some of the spoken language, in line with the principles of language acquisition, in which development of the listening and speaking skills comes before learning how to read and write. But students not yet very familiar with spoken Japanese can use the online audio files to familiarize themselves with native Japanese pronunciation of each symbol as it is introduced. As you study each character and sample words, listen, repeat, and listen again! Saying the words out loud helps you learn them, as well as polishing your Japanese pronunciation, so don't be shy about it.

Moving on

Students who have mastered the exercises in this book, and students who already have a working knowledge of Japanese grammar can build on their skills with further study materials that can be found on this book's online site. The audio files used in the book can also be accessed here, along with gridded paper for handwriting practice, and downloadable flashcards. Go to **www.tuttlepublishing.com/reading-and-writing-japanese-katakana**

An Introduction to Katakana

The Japanese writing system

The modern Japanese writing system combines three types of scripts: *kanji*, *hiragana*, and *katakana*. Kanji characters were originally borrowed from Chinese and adapted to fit Japanese. There are several thousand kanji and Japanese students are required to learn more than two thousand by the time they graduate from secondary school. Each kanji possesses multiple meanings and can have several pronunciations.

On the other hand, hiragana and katakana are syllabaries. Each symbol represents one syllabic unit of Japanese but possesses no inherent meaning. The hiragana and katakana syllabaries are comprised of 46 basic symbols, 25 symbols with diacritics, 33 contracted combinations, and some special representations. The katakana symbols were developed from simplified kanji, but they no longer bear any visible resemblance.

Written Japanese sentences combine kanji, hiragana and katakana in highly conventionalized ways to function as a comprehensive writing system. In addition, English alphabet letters and Arabic numerals may be mixed in too, as shown in this example:

デパートは、約 200m 先 です。

(bold = katakana; underlined = hiragana; ☐ = *kanji*)

The department store is about 200 meters ahead.

What is written in katakana?

Katakana is used mainly to represent foreign names and loanwords—Japanese words borrowed and adapted from a foreign language. Most loanwords these days come from English. Beginners will find it encouraging that they can understand many katakana words and expressions based solely on their knowledge of English. Given the global predominance of English as a common language, katakana vocabulary is rapidly expanding. Having a knowledge of katakana will enable learners to scan and extract target information from a wide range of authentic texts such as menus, schedules, maps, text messages, social media posts, signs, and articles to do with fashion and sports. In addition, learners will be able to read and write foreign names in katakana, including their own. Katakana is also used to write the following:

- Japanese words whose kanji are hard or rare
- Onomatopoeia and words that represent sounds or noises
- Emphasized words usually italicized in English
- Words spoken with an unusual accent, such as by foreigners or synthesized voices

What happens to a foreign word when borrowed into Japanese?

Many Japanese words and phrases are borrowed from other languages, particularly from English. When words are borrowed, they go through some changes. First, their pronunciation changes to fit the Japanese sound system. Second, these words typically become nouns in Japanese, regardless of what they were in their original language. Third, their meaning in Japanese may be different (for example, スマート **sumāto** which reads as "smart," but means slender). Fourth, they are usually written in katakana, though there are a few exceptions which use the English alphabet, such as "Wi-Fi," or "EU," for example.

If the original words or phrases are long, they are often abbreviated and can become very different from the original (for example, スマホ **sumaho** for smartphone). It's common to abbreviate two-word phrases by taking the first two syllables from each and combining them to make a four-syllable word (for example, セクハラ **sekuhara** for sexual harassment).

Vertical and horizontal writing

Modern Japanese can be written horizontally, from left to right, or vertically, from top to bottom starting from the right column and moving left. Due to editorial limitations, text is presented only horizontally in this book. Learners are encouraged to practice vertical writing and develop familiarity with it.

The basic 46 katakana symbols 🎧 Track 01

Japanese syllables are organized in the chart below, which is called the **gojūon-hyō**, meaning "the table of 50 sounds." This fixed order of syllables is used to organize dictionaries and other lists, similar to "alphabetical order" in English. The chart is ten columns wide and five rows high, it thus has 50 blocks. However, since not all blocks are filled, and the syllabic /**n**/ is extra, there are 46 basic syllables. The traditional chart used in Japanese schools is read from right to left, with the a, i, u, e, o row on the right-hand side of the chart. In this book the chart has been reversed for the benefit of Western readers, and should be read from top to bottom, left to right.

	k	s	t	n	h	m	y	r	w	
ア a	カ ka	サ sa	タ ta	ナ na	ハ ha	マ ma	ヤ ya	ラ ra	ワ wa	ン n
イ i	キ ki	シ shi	チ chi	ニ ni	ヒ hi	ミ mi		リ ri		
ウ u	ク ku	ス su	ツ tsu	ヌ nu	フ fu	ム mu	ユ yu	ル ru		
エ e	ケ ke	セ se	テ te	ネ ne	ヘ he	メ me		レ re		
オ o	コ ko	ソ so	ト to	ノ no	ホ ho	モ mo	ヨ yo	ロ ro	ヲ o	

Voiced sounds 🎧 Track 02

Diacritical marks can be added to certain syllables to indicate voiced or hardened sounds, known as **dakuon** in Japanese.

	g	z	d	b	p
a	ガ ga	ザ za	ダ da	バ ba	パ pa
i	ギ gi	ジ ji	ヂ ji	ビ bi	ピ pi
u	グ gu	ズ zu	ヅ zu	ブ bu	プ pu
e	ゲ ge	ゼ ze	デ de	ベ be	ペ pe
o	ゴ go	ゾ zo	ド do	ボ bo	ポ po

Contracted sounds 🎧 Track 03

There are 33 syllables that can be combined with /**ya**/, /**yu**/, or /**yo**/ to make contracted sounds, known as **yō-on** in Japanese. For example, /**ki**/ and /**ya**/ can be combined to make one syllable /**kya**/. Note in the chart below that the second syllable is written smaller, to indicate the combination. If the two syllables are the same size then they are treated as uncombined syllables, with the pronunciation of each given equal weight.

	ki	gi	shi	ji	chi	ni	hi	bi	pi	mi	ri
ya	kya キャ	gya ギャ	sha シャ	ja ジャ	cha チャ	nya ニャ	hya ヒャ	bya ビャ	pya ピャ	mya ミャ	rya リャ
yu	kyu キュ	gyu ギュ	shu シュ	ju ジュ	chu チュ	nyu ニュ	hyu ヒュ	byu ビュ	pyu ピュ	myu ミュ	ryu リュ
yo	kyo キョ	gyo ギョ	sho ショ	jo ジョ	cho チョ	nyo ニョ	hyo ヒョ	byo ビョ	pyo ピョ	myo ミョ	ryo リョ

Punctuation and other symbols

Several Japanese punctuation marks are introduced in this book.

。 This marks the end of a sentence like the period marks the end of an English sentence. In Japanese this is called *maru*.

、 This marks a break in a sentence, much like the comma in English. Note the direction of the symbol. It goes from top left to bottom right. In Japanese this is called *ten*.

• This "middle dot," called *nakaguro* in Japanese, is used in certain situations to separate katakana words, for example a family name from a given name. It takes the space of one whole katakana symbol. You can see examples of this usage on pages 83–85.

? This question mark is borrowed from English and typically used when the status of a sentence as a question is not clear due to the lack of the Japanese question marker /**ka**/ in casual speech.

! This exclamation mark is also borrowed from English.

The last two symbols have recently gained solid popularity in texting and other casual writing. However, they are not used in traditional writing and still rare in official documents.

PART 1

Reading and Writing Katakana: The Basics

A Column

a	say "<u>ah</u>"
i	"Wh<u>eee</u>!" This slide is fun!
u	use this sc<u>oo</u>p
e	<u>e</u>xercise with weights
o	a big old <u>oa</u>k tree

Long Vowels

A long vowel is held for two beats, the second beat represented by a bar.

ア ー **ā** like <u>ah</u>	ア ー					
イ ー **ī** like <u>ea</u>st	イ ー					
ウ ー **ū** like yah<u>oo</u>	ウ ー					
エ ー **ē** like b<u>ay</u>	エ ー					
オ ー **ō** like p<u>au</u>se	オ ー					

Writing Drill 1 🎧 Track 04

Read the samples, listen to the audio, and copy the words using the squares. Extra gridded paper for writing practice can be downloaded at the link on page 6.

eā air

エ	ア	ー									

uea wear

ウ	エ	ア									

ō oh; the letter O

オ	ー										

ē the letter A

エ	ー										

ī the letter E

イ	ー										

Ka Column

ka — "Caw! Caw!" says the crow

ki — a mysterious key

ku — I'm writing a haiku

ke — time to do some chemistry

ko — a sleepy koala

Ga Column

When two dots are added, /**k**/ becomes /**g**/.

ガ **ga**	ガ	ガ						
ギ **gi**	ギ	ギ						
グ **gu**	グ	グ						
ゲ **ge**	ゲ	ゲ						
ゴ **go**	ゴ	ゴ						

Writing Drill 2 🎧 Track 05

Read the samples, listen to the audio, and copy the words using the squares.

eko ecology

エ	コ										

kī key

キ	ー										

kā car

カ	ー										

kēki cake

ケ	ー	キ												

ōku oak

オ	ー	ク												

kea care

ケ	ア	ー												

akua aqua

ア	ク	ア												

ego ego

エ	ゴ																

gia gear

ギ	ア																

ēge The Aegean Sea

エ	ー	ゲ										

koa core

コ	ア																

Sa Column

sa

There's a flying <u>sa</u>ucer!

shi

a delicious piece of su<u>shi</u>

su

I'm going to pur<u>sue</u> the culprit

se

<u>se</u>t that down carefully

so

catch these <u>so</u>ap bubbles

Za Column

When two dots are added, unvoiced sounds become voiced.

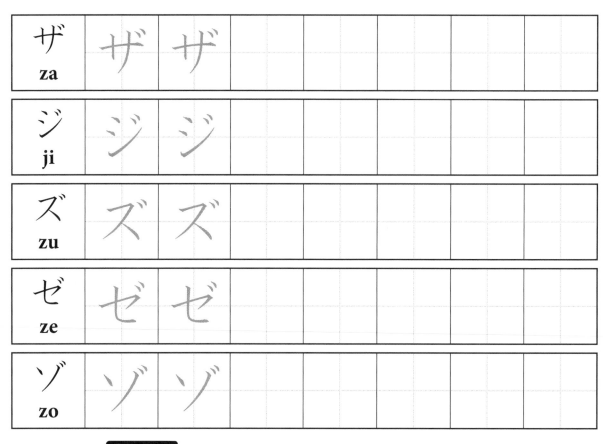

Writing Drill 3 🎧 Track 06

Read the samples, listen to the audio, and copy the words using the squares.

aisu ice

アイス

ēsu ace

エース

sukī skiing

スキー

saizu size

サイズ

sōsu sauce

ソース

shī the letter C

シー

iesu yes; Jesus

イエス

shikago Chicago

シカゴ

akusesu access

アクセス

ajia Asia

アジア

gasu gas

ガス

kōsu course

コース

oashisu oasis

オアシス

sōsēji sausage

ソーセージ

katsu cutlet

カツ

jiguzagu zigzag

ジグザグ

sākasu circus

サーカス

uesuto kōsuto West Coast

ウエストコースト

Ta Column

ta	a little be<u>tta</u> fish	タ	タ	タ	タ
chi	I love <u>chee</u>se	チ	チ	チ	チ
tsu	that guy knows juji<u>tsu</u>	ツ	ツ	ツ	ツ
te	your <u>ta</u>ble is over there	テ	テ	テ	テ
to	let's have a <u>to</u>ast	ト	ト	ト	ト

Da Column

When two dots are added, the unvoiced sounds become voiced.

Writing Drill 4 🎧 Track 07

Read the samples, listen to the audio, and copy the words using the squares.

kētai cell phone

ケ	ー	タ	イ

doa door

ド	ア

takushī taxi

タ	ク	シ	ー

dēta data

デ	ー	タ

sutēki steak

ステーキ

chīzu cheese

チーズ

shītsu sheet

シーツ

tai Thailand

タイ

sutāto start

スタート

sutoa store

ストア

tōsuto toast

トースト

tesuto test

テスト

sōda soda

ソーダ

sutajio studio

スタジオ

gitā guitar

ギター

āto art

アート

gēto gate

ゲート

Na Column

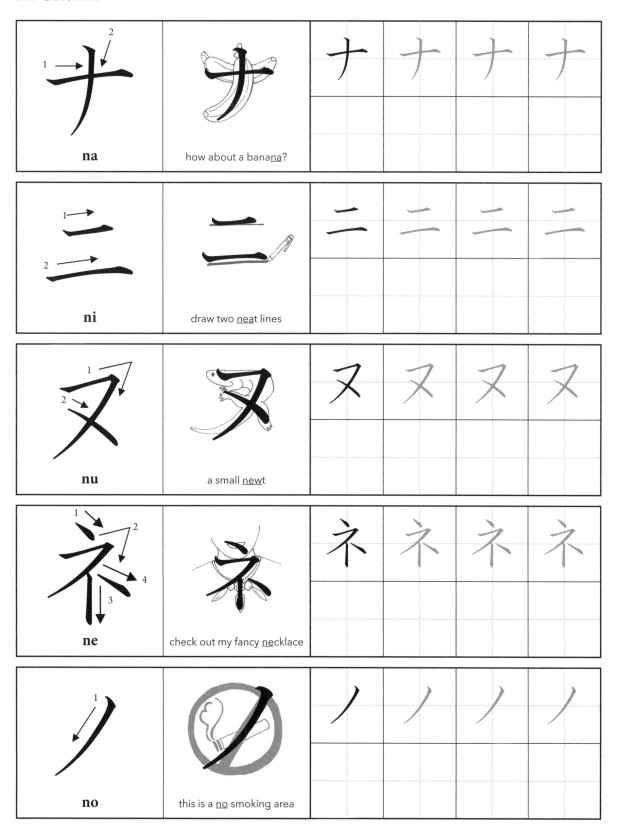

na	how about a bana<u>na</u>?				
ni	draw two <u>nea</u>t lines				
nu	a small <u>new</u>t				
ne	check out my fancy <u>ne</u>cklace				
no	this is a <u>no</u> smoking area				

Writing Drill 5 🎧 Track 08

Read the samples, listen to the audio, and copy the words using the squares.

nō no

ノ	ー										

nau now

ナ	ウ										

kanada Canada

カ	ナ	ダ					

naiki Nike

ナ	イ	キ					

nōto note

ノ	ー	ト					

tenisu tennis

テ	ニ	ス					

naisu nice

ナ	イ	ス					

kone connection

コ	ネ								

ōnā owner

オ	ー	ナ	ー				

kanū canoe

カ	ヌ	ー					

sonī Sony

ソ	ニ	ー					

tsuna tuna

ツ	ナ										

Ha Column

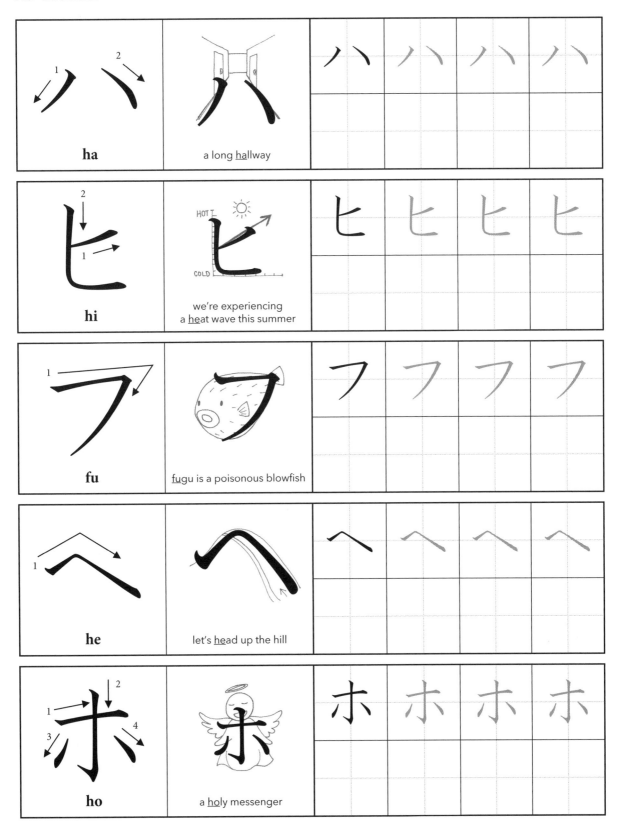

ha	a long <u>ha</u>llway
hi	we're experiencing a <u>he</u>at wave this summer
fu	<u>fu</u>gu is a poisonous blowfish
he	let's <u>he</u>ad up the hill
ho	a <u>ho</u>ly messenger

When two dots are added, /h/ becomes /b/.

バ ba	バ	バ						
ビ bi	ビ	ビ						
ブ bu	ブ	ブ						
ベ be	ベ	ベ						
ボ bo	ボ	ボ						

When a small circle is added, /h/ becomes /p/.

パ pa	パ	パ						
ピ pi	ピ	ピ						
プ pu	プ	プ						
ペ pe	ペ	ペ						
ポ po	ポ	ポ						

Writing Drill 6 🎧 Track 09

Read the samples, listen to the audio, and copy the words using the squares.

kōhī coffee

コ ー ヒ ー

basu bus

バ ス

haiteku hi-tech

ハ イ テ ク

sūpā supermarket

ス ー パ ー

kopī copy

コ ピ ー

pasupōto passport

パ ス ポ ー ト

hōru hall; hole

ホ ー ル

tēburu table

テ ー ブ ル

bebī baby

ベ ビ ー

sutaba Starbucks

ス タ バ

naifu knife

ナ イ フ

baito student worker; part-time worker

バ イ ト

Ma Column

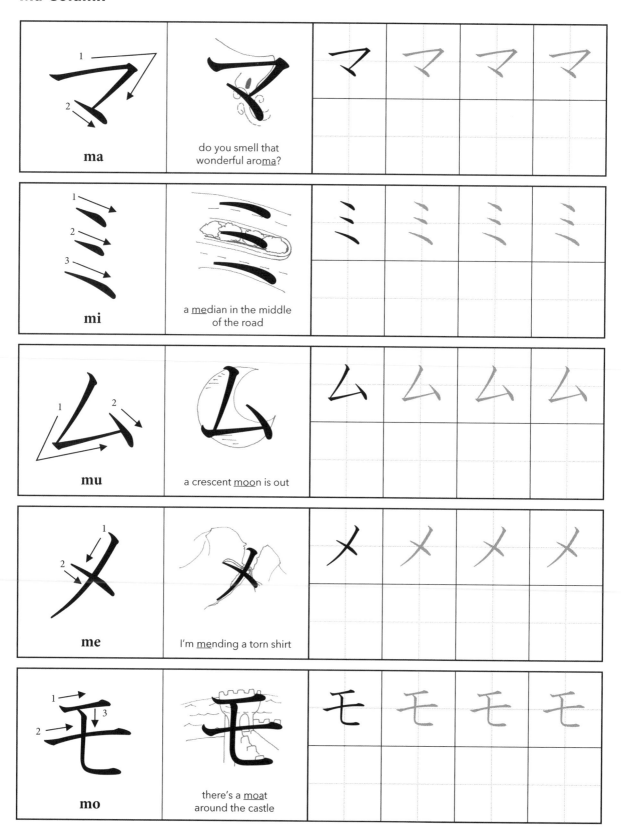

ma

do you smell that wonderful ar<u>oma</u>?

mi

a <u>me</u>dian in the middle of the road

mu

a crescent <u>moo</u>n is out

me

I'm <u>me</u>nding a torn shirt

mo

there's a <u>moa</u>t around the castle

Writing Drill 7 🎧 Track 10

Read the samples, listen to the audio, and copy the words using the squares.

sumaho smart phone

スマホ

hōmu home

ホーム

gēmu game

ゲーム

taimu time

タイム

manā manner

マナー

pāto taimu part time

パートタイム

masukomi media; mass communication

マスコミ

jimu gym

ジム

obama Obama

オバマ

mama mother

ママ

mīto meat

ミート

hamu ham

ハム

Ya Column

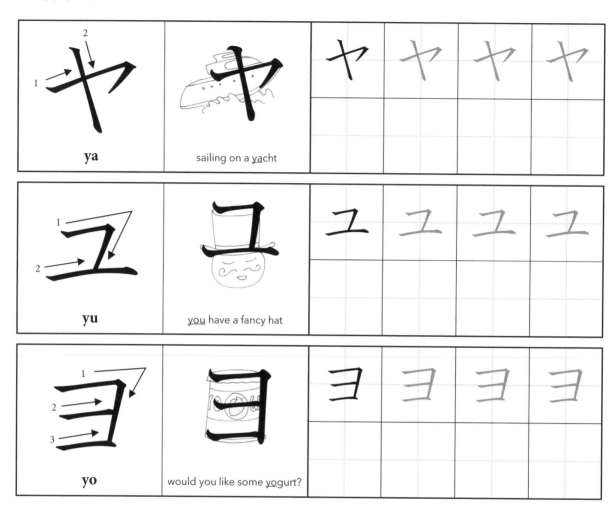

ya	sailing on a <u>ya</u>cht		
yu	<u>you</u> have a fancy hat		
yo	would you like some <u>yo</u>gurt?		

Writing Drill 8 🎧 Track 11

Read the samples, listen to the audio, and copy the words using the squares.

iyā year; ear

イ ヤ ー

taiya tire

タ イ ヤ

yū the letter U

ユ ー

yoga yoga

ヨ ガ

Wa Column

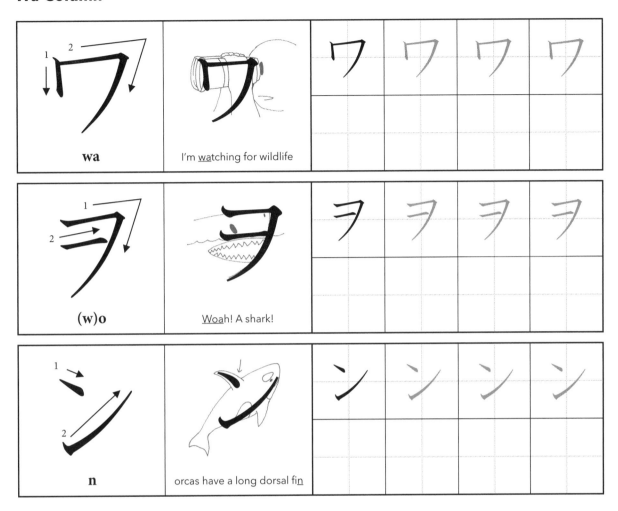

wa	I'm <u>wa</u>tching for wildlife	ワ	ワ	ワ	ワ
(w)o	<u>Wo</u>ah! A shark!	ヲ	ヲ	ヲ	ヲ
n	orcas have a long dorsal fi<u>n</u>	ン	ン	ン	ン

Writing Drill 9   🎧 Track 12

Read the samples, listen to the audio, and copy the words using the squares.

washinton Washington

ワ	シ	ン	ト	ン											

pasokon PC; personal computer

パ	ソ	コ	ン												

wādo Word (software)

ワ	ー	ド													

wain wine

ワ	イ	ン													

Ra Column

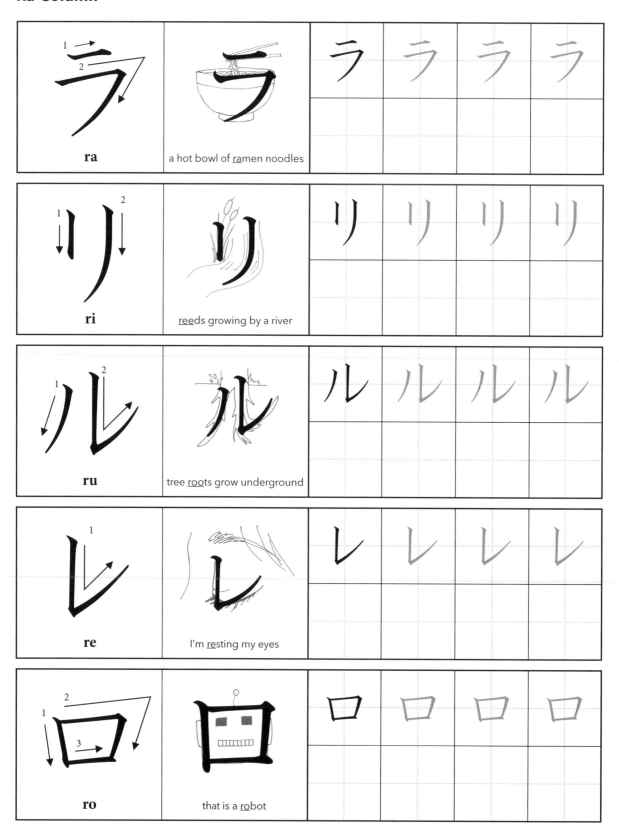

ra — a hot bowl of <u>ra</u>men noodles

ri — <u>ree</u>ds growing by a river

ru — tree <u>roo</u>ts grow underground

re — I'm <u>re</u>sting my eyes

ro — that is a <u>ro</u>bot

Writing Drill 10 🎧 Track 13

Read the samples, listen to the audio, and copy the words using the squares.

rate latte

ラ テ

kurisumasu Christmas

ク リ ス マ ス

doru dollar

ド ル

bīru beer

ビ ー ル

mōru mall

モ ー ル

toire toilet

ト イ レ

erebētā elevator

エ レ ベ ー タ ー

esukarētā escalator

エ ス カ レ ー タ ー

yūro Euro

ユ ー ロ

harō hello

ハ ロ ー

isuramu Islam

イ ス ラ ム

itaria Italy

イ タ リ ア

Contracted Sounds

Contracted sounds combine the /i/ form of a katakana syllable with /ya/, /yu/ or /yo/. To indicate this contracted sound, /ya/, /yu/ and /yo/ are written small.

kya

キ ャ			

kyu

キ ュ			

kyo

キ ョ			

gya

ギ ャ			

gyu

ギ ュ			

gyo

ギ ョ			

sha

シ ャ			

shu

シ ュ			

sho

シ ョ			

ja

ジ ャ			

ju

ジ ュ			

jo

ジ ョ			

cha

チ ャ			

chu

チ ュ			

cho

チ ョ			

nya

ニ ャ			

nyu

ニ ュ			

nyo

ニ ョ			

hya

ヒ ャ			

hyu

ヒ ュ			

hyo

ヒ ョ			

bya

ビ ャ			

byu

ビ ュ			

byo

ビ ョ			

pya

ピ ャ			

pyu

ピ ュ			

pyo

ピ ョ			

mya

ミ ャ			

myu

ミ ュ			

myo

ミ ョ			

rya

リ ャ			

ryu

リ ュ			

ryo

リ ョ			

Writing Drill 11 🎧 Track 14

Read the samples, listen to the audio, and copy the words using the squares.

kyanseru cancel

| キ | ャ | ン | セ | ル |

kyasshu cash

| キ | ャ | ッ | シ | ュ |

kyūba Cuba

| キ | ュ | ー | バ |

gyappu gap

| ギ | ャ | ッ | プ |

shatsu shirt

| シ | ャ | ツ |

shūzu shoes

| シ | ュ | ー | ズ |

mochibēshon motivation

| モ | チ | ベ | ー | シ | ョ | ン |

manshon condominium

| マ | ン | シ | ョ | ン |

tenshon anticipation

| テ | ン | シ | ョ | ン |

shoppingu shopping

| シ | ョ | ッ | ピ | ン | グ |

jazu jazz

| ジ | ャ | ズ |

jūsu juice

| ジ | ュ | ー | ス |

jogingu jogging

| ジ | ョ | ギ | ン | グ | | | | | | | | | | | |

chatto chat

| チ | ャ | ッ | ト | | | | | | | | | | | | |

chū kiss

| チ | ュ | ー | | | | | | | | | | | | | |

magunichūdo magnitude

| マ | グ | ニ | チ | ュ | ー | ド | | | | | | | | | |

chokorēto chocolate

| チ | ョ | コ | レ | ー | ト | | | | | | | | | | |

nyūsu news

| ニ | ュ | ー | ス | | | | | | | | | | | | |

nyūyōku New York

| ニ | ュ | ー | ヨ | ー | ク | | | | | | | | | | |

hyūman human

| ヒ | ュ | ー | マ | ン | | | | | | | | | | | |

pyonyan Pyongyang

| ピ | ョ | ン | ヤ | ン | | | | | | | | | | | |

myanmā Myanmar

| ミ | ャ | ン | マ | ー | | | | | | | | | | | |

myūjikku music

| ミ | ュ | ー | ジ | ッ | ク | | | | | | | | | | |

ryukku rucksack

| リ | ュ | ッ | ク | | | | | | | | | | | | |

ryūmachi rheumatism

| リ | ュ | ー | マ | チ | | | | | | | | | | | |

Long Consonants

A small ツ before a syllable has the effect of doubling the sound of that syllable to form a "long consonant." Traditionally the only consonants that could be doubled in this way were the voiceless /**k**/, /**s**/, /**t**/ and /**p**/, but recently innovative pronunciations have emerged and small ツ is also used to double the voiced consonants /**g**/, /**z**/, /**d**/, and /**b**/.

When writing horizontally, small ツ is written in the bottom left hand corner. When writing vertically it is written in the top right hand corner.

Writing Drill 12 🎧 Track 15

Read the samples, listen to the audio, and copy the words using the squares.

netto Internet; net

ネ ッ ト

koppu cup; glass

コ ッ プ

getto get

ゲ ッ ト

setto set

セ ッ ト

sakkā soccer

サ ッ カ ー

sokkusu socks

ソ ッ ク ス

appurōdo upload

アップロード

tsuittā Twitter

ツイッター

kurejitto kādo credit card

クレジットカード

orinpikku Olympics

オリンピック

rokkā locker

ロッカー

chiketto ticket

チケット

beddo bed

ベッド

kizzu kids

キッズ

baggu bag

バッグ

eggu egg

エッグ

biggu makku Big Mac

ビッグマック

guddo rakku good luck

グッドラック

doraggu sutoa drugstore

ドラッグストア

Innovative Pronunciations

Generally, when a foreign word is borrowed into Japanese, its original pronunciation is altered to fit the Japanese phonological system and is written in katakana from the traditional charts shown in this introduction. However, more recently borrowed words tend to be pronounced and written to better reflect their original pronunciation, resulting in new combinations of katakana that did not exist before. The following have become part of standard Japanese:

ti

ティ			

di

ディ			

she

シェ			

je

ジェ			

che

チェ			

fa

ファ			

fi

フィ			

fe

フェ			

fo

フォ			

va

ヴァ			

vi

ヴィ			

vu

ヴ			

ve

ヴェ			

vo

ヴォ			

wi   **we**   **wo**

ウィ		ウェ		ウォ	

Writing Drill 13 🎧 Track 16

media media

メ	ディ	ア					

shefu chef

シ	ェ	フ					

jetto jet

ジェット

chero cello

チェロ

firumu film

フィルム

byuffe buffet; all you can eat

ビュッフェ

kariforunia California

カリフォルニア

vaiorin violin

ヴァイオリン

vīnasu Venus

ヴィーナス

kurisumasu ivu Christmas Eve

クリスマスイヴ

venisu Venice

ヴェニス

vōkaru vocal

ヴォーカル

harowin Halloween

ハロウィーン

webu peeji webpage

ウェブページ

wooku walk

ウォーク

PART 2

Reading and Writing Katakana: Vocabulary Practice

Food and Drink

piza pizza

ピ ザ

furai fried food

フ ラ イ

karē curry

カ レ ー

sarada salad

サ ラ ダ

chīzu cheese

チ ー ズ

pasuta pasta

パ ス タ

bīfu beef

ビ ー フ

chikin chicken

チ キ ン

tōsuto toast

ト ー ス ト

rāmen ramen

ラ ー メ ン

gyōza gyoza dumpling

ギ ョ ー ザ

omuretsu omelet

オ ム レ ツ

supagettī spaghetti

スパゲッティー

guratan gratin

グラタン

korokke croquette

コロッケ

kechappu ketchup

ケチャップ

tsuna sando tuna sandwich

ツナサンド

chāhan fried rice

チャーハン

omuraisu rice omelet

オムライス

shī fūdo seafood

シーフード

hanbāgā hamburger

ハンバーガー

furaido potato French fries

フライドポテト

potechi potato chips

ポテチ

kēki cake

ケーキ

kukkī cookie

クッキー

dezāto dessert

デザート

kasutera sponge cake

カステラ

chokorēto chocolate

チョコレート

aisu kurīmu ice cream

アイスクリーム

rate latte

ラテ

kōra cola

コーラ

jūsu juice

ジュース

sumūjī smoothie

スムージー

sutoroberī strawberry

ストロベリー

aisu kōhī ice coffee

アイスコーヒー

bīru beer

ビール

wain wine

ワイン

ranchi setto lunch set

ランチセット

Reading and Writing Practice

Extra gridded paper for writing practice can be downloaded at the link on page 6.

I.   Circle the item that does not belong in each group. Check your answers on page 93.

Group A	Group B	Group C	Group D	Group E
コーラ	ケーキ	ラーメン	カステラ	カレー
アイスクリーム	グラタン	ハンバーガー	チョコレート	チャーハン
ジュース	コロッケ	サラダ	クッキー	ピザ
アイスコーヒー	パスタ	サンドイッチ	アイスクリーム	ポテトサラダ
スムージー	カレー	ケチャップ	ビーフ	ワイン

II. Listen to audio track 18. Write the words you hear in katakana. Check your answers on page 93. All audio files can be found on this book's website at the link on page 6.

1. _____   6. _____

2. _____   7. _____

3. _____   8. _____

4. _____   9. _____

5. _____   10. _____

III. Keiko is taking lunch orders for her group. Listen to her confirm everyone's order on audio track 19 and write in katakana what the people below are having. Answers are on page 93.

1. Ms. Tanaka   _____

2. Ms. Sato   _____

3. Ms. Nakamura   _____

4. Arisa   _____

5. Naomi   _____

IV. Write a list of your favorite food chosen from the lists on pages 42–44.

In Town

biru building

| ビ | ル | | | | | | | | |

depāto department store

| デ | パ | ー | ト | | | |

mōru shopping mall

| モ | ー | ル | | | | |

konbini convenience store

| コ | ン | ビ | ニ | | | |

sūpā supermarket

| ス | ー | パ | ー | | | |

gasorin sutando gas station

| ガ | ソ | リ | ン | ス | タ | ン | ド | | |

kafe café

| カ | フ | ェ | | | | |

netto kafe Internet café

| ネ | ッ | ト | カ | フ | ェ | | |

kōhī shoppu coffee shop

| コ | ー | ヒ | ー | ショ | ッ | プ | |

fāsuto fūdo fast food

| フ | ァ | ー | ス | ト | フ | ー | ド | |

resutoran restaurant

| レ | ス | ト | ラ | ン | | |

famiresu family restaurant

| フ | ァ | ミ | レ | ス | | |

bā bar

バー

bia gāden beer garden

ビアガーデン

gēmu sentā game arcade

ゲームセンター

koin randorī laundromat

コインランドリー

kurīningu dry cleaner

クリーニング

komyunitī sentā community center

コミュニティーセンター

pākingu parking

パーキング

pāku park

パーク

jimu gym

ジム

supōtsu kurabu sports club

スポーツクラブ

erebētā elevator

エレベーター

esukarētā escalator

エスカレーター

ion Aeon (shopping mall)

イオン

paruko Parco (shopping mall)

パ ル コ

rumine Lumine (shopping mall)

ル ミ ネ

rōson Lawson

ロ ー ソ ン

sebun irebun Seven Eleven

セ ブ ン イ レ ブ ン

famirī māto Family Mart

フ ァ ミ リ ー マ ー ト

sutābakkusu Starbucks

ス タ ー バ ッ ク ス

makudonarudo McDonald's

マ ク ド ナ ル ド

wendīzu Wendy's

ウ ェ ン デ ェ ー ズ

mosubāgā Mos Burger

モ ス バ ー ガ ー

sabuwēi Subway

サ ブ ウ ェ イ

misutā dōnatsu Mister Donut

ミ ス タ ー ド ー ナ ツ

kentakkī KFC

ケ ン タ ッ キ ー

denīzu Denny's

デ ニ ー ズ

Reading and Writing Practice

I.   Circle the item that does not belong in each group. Check your answers on page 93.

Group A	Group B	Group C	Group D	Group E
ショップ	コンサートホール	ジュース	パルコ	ネットカフェ
デパート	ビジネスセンター	ワインバー	イオン	ドーナツ
ビール	スポーツクラブ	コーヒーショップ	コーヒー	デニーズ
スーパー	パーク	ビアガーデン	デパート	マクドナルド
コンビニ	ゲームセンター	レストラン	モール	ローソン

II.   Listen to audio track 21. Write the words you hear in katakana. Answers are on page 93.

1. _____   6. _____

2. _____   7. _____

3. _____   8. _____

4. _____   9. _____

5. _____   10. _____

III. Listen to audio track 22 and write where the person went. Check your answers on page 93.

Example: メリーさんは、デパートにいきました。
           Merī-san wa, depāto ni ikimashita.   Mary went to the department store.
Answer: デパート

1. Mary   デパート _____   4. Teresa   _____

2. Emily   _____   5. Mei Mei   _____

3. Ito-san   _____   6. Mr. Moti   _____

IV.   Which places mentioned on pages 46–48 do you have in your neighborhood? Make a list.

House and Home

manshon condo; upscale apartment

マ ン シ ョ ン

apāto apartment

ア パ ー ト

tawā-manshon high-rise condo

タ ワ ー マ ン シ ョ ン

shea hausu shared house

シ ェ ア ハ ウ ス

kicchin kitchen

キ ッ チ ン

ribingu living room

リ ビ ン グ

dainingu dining room

ダ イ ニ ン グ

beddo rūmu bedroom

ベ ッ ド ル ー ム

basu rūmu bathroom

バ ス ル ー ム

toire toilet

ト イ レ

doa door

ド ア

interia interior

イ ン テ リ ア

beranda porch

ベ ラ ン ダ

garasu glass (window)

ガ ラ ス

terebi TV

テ レ ビ

eakon air conditioner

エ ア コ ン

hītā heater

ヒ ー タ ー

sutando table lamp

ス タ ン ド

beddo bed

ベ ッ ド

tēburu table

テ ー ブ ル

sofa sofa

ソ フ ァ

surippa slippers

ス リ ッ パ

kāpetto carpet

カ ー ペ ッ ト

kusshon cushion

ク ッ シ ョ ン

kāten curtain

カ ー テ ン

shītsu bed sheet

シ ー ツ

taoru towel

タ オ ル

shanpū shampoo

シ ャ ン プ ー

kondishonā conditioner

コ ン デ ィ シ ョ ナ ー

toiretto pēpā toilet paper

ト イ レ ッ ト ・ ペ ー パ ー

tisshu tissue

テ ィ ッ シ ュ

naifu knife

ナ イ フ

fōku fork

フ ォ ー ク

supūn spoon

ス プ ー ン

koppu cup (glass)

コ ッ プ

kappu cup (non-glass)

カ ッ プ

gurasu glass (for drinks)

グ ラ ス

renji stove; microwave oven

レ ン ジ

Reading and Writing Practice

I.   Circle the item that does not belong in each group. Check your answers on page 93.

Group A	Group B	Group C	Group D	Group E
ヒーター	スタンド	コーヒーカップ	アパート	ラーメン
シーツ	ベッド	ヒーター	スーパー	チーズトースト
クッション	テーブル	エアコン	マンション	サラダ
カーテン	タオル	テレビ	コンビニ	シャンプー
カーペット	ソファ	レンジ	ティッシュ	アイスクリーム

II.   Listen to audio track 24. Write the words you hear in katakana. Answers are on page 93.

1. _____   6. _____

2. _____   7. _____

3. _____   8. _____

4. _____   9. _____

5. _____   10. _____

III. Where in a house do you typically find the following items? Write your answer in katakana. Check your answers on page 93.

1. シーツ   _____

2. コンディショナー   _____

3. テレビ   _____

4. レンジ   _____

5. ソファ   _____

IV.   You are helping a friend settle into a new apartment. Listen to audio track 25 and make a shopping list in katakana of the things she needs. Check your answers on page 93.

V.   What kind of housing do you live in? What rooms, furniture, and household items do you have? Write them in katakana only if they are commonly written in katakana.

IT and Communications

komyunikēshon communication

コ　ミュ　ニ　ケ　ー　ショ　ン

tekunorojī technology

テ　ク　ノ　ロ　ジ　ー

haiteku hi-tech

ハ　イ　テ　ッ　ク

media media

メ　ディ　ア

netto Internet

ネ　ッ　ト

kētai cellphone

ケ　ー　タ　イ

sumaho smartphone

ス　マ　ホ

apuri app

ア　プ　リ

konpyūtā computer

コ　ン　ピュ　ー　タ　ー

pasokon PC

パ　ソ　コ　ン

nōto pasokon laptop computer

ノ　ー　ト　パ　ソ　コ　ン

taburetto tablet

タ　ブ　レ　ッ　ト

sofuto software

ソフト

mēru email; text message

メール

meado email address

メアド

gūguru Google

グーグル

feisubukku Facebook

フェイスブック

tsuittā Twitter

ツイッター

insuta Instagram

インスタ

yūchūbu YouTube

ユーチューブ

appuru Apple

アップル

yūzā user

ユーザー

forowā follower

フォロワー

akaunto account

アカウント

roguin login

ログイン

pasuwādo password

パスワード

kurikku click

クリック

daunrōdo download

ダウンロード

appu upload

アップ

posuto post

ポスト

kopipe copy and paste

コピペ

onrain online

オンライン

puraibashī privacy

プライバシー

sekyuritī security

セキュリティー

appudēto update

アップデート

hōmupēji homepage

ホームページ

saito website

サイト

purofīru profile

プロフィール

Reading and Writing Practice

I.   Circle the item that does not belong in each group. Check your answers on page 93.

Group A	Group B	Group C	Group D	Group E
スマホ	セキュリティー	クリック	セブンイレブン	プライバシー
カーテン	フェイスブック	ポスト	グーグル	フレンド
タブレット	インスタ	ログイン	トヨタ	オバマ
パソコン	ユーチューブ	アップ	パスワード	ユーザー
ケータイ	ツイッター	グレープ	マクドナルド	フォロワー

II. Listen to audio track 27. Write the words you hear in katakana. Answers are on page 94.

1. _____   6. _____

2. _____   7. _____

3. _____   8. _____

4. _____   9. _____

5. _____   10. _____

III. Write two examples of each category under the heading. Check your answers on page 94.

Social Media	Digital Device	US Hi-Tech Company

IV. Your team is having some computer problems (*mondai*). Listen to audio track 28 and write the name of the problem that is being talked about. Check your answers on page 94.

1. _____   4. _____

2. _____   5. _____

3. _____

V.   Which devices, sites or apps listed on pages 54–55 do you use? Make a list in katakana.

Transport and Tourism

takushī taxi

タクシー

basu bus

バス

monorēru monorail

モノレール

rentakā rental car

レンタカー

maikā my car (privately owned car)

マイカー

ōtobai motorcycle

オートバイ

baiku motorcycle

バイク

ferī ferry

フェリー

metoro Metro (subway)

メトロ

ekusupuresu express

エクスプレス

sukairainā Skyliner

スカイライナー

tonneru tunnel

トンネル

basu tāminaru bus terminal

バスターミナル

hōmu platform

ホーム

koin rokkā coin locker

コインロッカー

japan rēru pasu Japan Rail Pass

ジャパン・レールパス

shatoru basu shuttle bus

シャトルバス

furaito flight

フライト

gēto gate

ゲート

kauntā counter

カウンター

pasupōto passport

パスポート

biza visa

ビザ

chiketto ticket

チケット

kiyosuku kiosk

キヨスク

gaido bukku guide book

ガイドブック

kyarī baggu carry-on bag; roller luggage

キャリーバッグ

hoteru hotel

ホテル

bijinesu hoteru business hotel

ビジネスホテル

rizōto resort

リゾート

penshon lodge

ペンション

shinguru single

シングル

daburu double

ダブル

rūmu sābisu room service

ルームサービス

baikingu buffet; all-you-can-eat

バイキング

chekku in check in

チェックイン

chekku auto check out

チェックアウト

basu tsuā bus tour

バスツアー

bijitā sentā visitor center

ビジターセンター

Reading and Writing Practice

I.   Circle the item that does not belong in each group. Check your answers on page 94.

Group A	Group B	Group C	Group D	Group E
バスツアー	ホテル	メトロ	パスポート	ラウンジ
キッチン	ロッジ	トラベル	メール	ロビー
ベッドルーム	ペンション	タクシー	チケット	カウンター
トイレ	リゾート	バス	キャリーバッグ	バイク
リビング	フライト	モノレール	ビザ	ゲート

II. Listen to audio track 30. Write the words you hear in katakana. Answers are on page 94.

1. _____   6. _____

2. _____   7. _____

3. _____   8. _____

4. _____   9. _____

5. _____   10. _____

III. You are making travel plans with friends. Listen to audio track 31 and write the destination and the means of transport in the chart below. Check your answers on page 94.

Example: デパートまでバスでいきます。
              Depāto made basu de ikimasu.
              You get to the department store by bus.

Destination	Means of Transportation
1. デパート	バス
2.	
3.	
4.	
5.	

IV. Study the words for means of transportation on page 58. Which forms of transport do you prefer? Which do you dislike? Which have you never taken? Which would you like to take? Make lists in katakana.

Shopping

doru dollar

ド | ル

yūro Euro

ユ | ー | ロ

kurejitto kādo credit card

ク | レ | ジ | ッ | ト | カ | ー | ド

gifuto kādo gift certificate

ギ | フ | ト | カ | ー | ド

kyasshuresu cashless

キ | ャ | ッ | シ | ュ | レ | ス

bitto koin Bitcoin

ビ | ッ | ト | コ | イ | ン

netto shoppingu online shopping

ネ | ッ | ト | シ | ョ | ッ | ピ | ン | グ

ōkushon auction

オ | ー | ク | シ | ョ | ン

amazon Amazon

ア | マ | ゾ | ン

depāto department store

デ | パ | ー | ト

risaikuru shoppu second-hand shop

リ | サ | イ | ク | ル | シ | ョ | ッ | プ

reshīto receipt

レ | シ | ー | ト

shoppingu baggu shopping bag

ショッピングバッグ

dūtī furī duty-free

デューティーフリー

disukaunto discount

ディスカウント

bikku kamera Bic Camera (discount electronics store)

ビックカメラ

furoa gaido floor plan

フロアガイド

sābisu kauntā customer service

サービスカウンター

menzu men's clothing

メンズ

redīsu women's clothing

レディース

fasshon fashion

ファッション

fōmaru formal (clothing)

フォーマル

kajuaru casual

カジュアル

autodoa outdoor

アウトドア

bebī baby

ベビー

matanitī maternity

マ　タ　ニ　ティ　ー

akusesarī accessories

ア　ク　セ　サ　リ　ー

kosume cosmetics

コ　ス　メ

megane eye glasses

メ　ガ　ネ

supōtsu wea sportswear

ス　ポ　ー　ツ　ウェ　ア

baggu bag

バ　ッ　グ

gifuto gift

ギ　フ　ト

burando brand

ブ　ラ　ン　ド

butikku boutique

ブ　ティ　ッ　ク

saizu size

サ　イ　ズ

reji kauntā cashier

レ　ジ　カ　ウ　ン　タ　ー

serufu reji self-checkout

セ　ル　フ　レ　ジ

bākōdo barcode

バ　ー　コ　ー　ド

Reading and Writing Practice

I.   Circle the item that does not belong in each group. Check your answers on page 94.

Group A	Group B	Group C	Group D	Group E
デザート	メンズ	レシート	メガネ	セール
ハムサンド	クレジットカード	デパート	シューズ	バーゲン
ピザ	フォーマル	ネットショップ	バッグ	ディスカウント
Mサイズ	スポーツウェア	スーパー	ユーロ	ホテル
オムライス	マタニティー	コンビニ	コスメ	キャッシュレス

II.   Listen to audio track 33. Write the words you hear in katakana. Answers are on page 94.

1. _____   6. _____

2. _____   7. _____

3. _____   8. _____

4. _____   9. _____

5. _____   10. _____

III. Listen to audio track 34 and write in katakana the items purchased and where they were purchased. Check your answers on page 94.

Example: ギフトはデパートでかいました。
                Gifuto wa depāto de kaimashita.
                I bought the gift at the department store.

Item	Place of Purchase
1. ギフト	デパート
2.	
3.	
4.	
5.	

IV.   Have you been to a department store lately? Look at the vocabulary words on pages 63–64 and make a list of the departments you visited.

Business and Workplace 🎧 Track 35

bijinesu business

ビジネス

sararīman white-collar worker (male)

サラリーマン

gurōbaru global

グローバル

intānashonaru international

インターナショナル

sapurai chēn supply chain

サプライ・チェーン

fainansu finance

ファイナンス

māketingu marketing

マーケティング

operēshon operation

オペレーション

rojisutikusu logistics

ロジスティクス

kōporēshon corporation

コーポレーション

benchā startup company

ベンチャー

ofisu office

オフィス

chīmu team

チーム

manējimento management

マネージメント

rīdā leader

リーダー

intān intern

インターン

baito part-time student worker

バイト

pāto part-time worker

パート

ōeru OL (office lady), female office worker

オーエル

gabanansu governance

ガバナンス

manpawā manpower

マンパワー

chīmuwāku teamwork

チームワーク

kasutamā customer

カスタマー

kuraianto client

クライアント

baiyā buyer

バイヤー

sutēkuhorudā stakeholder

ステークホルダー

raibaru rival

ライバル

purojekuto project

プロジェクト

sukejūru schedule

スケジュール

mītingu meeting

ミーティング

apo appointment

アポ

purezen presentation

プレゼン

repōto report

レポート

furekkusu taimu flex time

フレックスタイム

inobēshon innovation

イノベーション

fīdobakku feedback

フィードバック

ofureko off the record

オフレコ

rejume resume

レジュメ

Reading and Writing Practice

I.   Circle the item that does not belong in each group. Check your answers on page 94.

Group A	Group B	Group C	Group D	Group E
パート	アポ	オフィス	クライアント	マーケティング
バイト	レポート	ビル	ライバル	ロジスティクス
インターン	ミーティング	オフレコ	グローバル	オペレーション
リーダー	ライバル	ロビー	サラリーマン	ファイナンス
フレックスタイム	プレゼン	ラウンジ	カスタマー	バイヤー

II.   Listen to audio track 36. Write the words you hear in katakana. Answers are on page 95.

1. _____   6. _____

2. _____   7. _____

3. _____   8. _____

4. _____   9. _____

5. _____   10. _____

III.   Listen to audio track 37. Your boss has some questions about a business meeting you attended. The particle は (**wa**) is used to mark the subject word of each question. Write the subject word of each question in katakana. Check your answers on page 95.

Example: マーケティングは？
             Māketingu wa?   What about the marketing?
Answer: マーケティング

1. マーケティング _____   6. _____

2. _____   7. _____

3. _____   8. _____

4. _____   9. _____

5. _____   10. _____

IV.   Which of the business and workplace terms on pages 66–68 do you use in your daily life? Write them in katakana.

Places in the World 🎧 Track 38

wārudo world

ワ ー ル ド

ajia Asia

ア ジ ア

yōroppa Europe

ヨ ー ロ ッ パ

afurika Africa

ア フ リ カ

amerika America

ア メ リ カ

kanada Canada

カ ナ ダ

igirisu England; Great Britain

イ ギ リ ス

ōsutoraria Australia

オ ー ス ト ラ リ ア

nyūjīrando New Zealand

ニ ュ ー ジ ー ラ ン ド

furansu France

フ ラ ン ス

doitsu Germany

ド イ ツ

roshia Russia

ロ シ ア

itaria Italy

イ タ リ ア

supein Spain

ス ペ イ ン

girisha Greece

ギ リ シ ャ

porutogaru Portugal

ポ ル ト ガ ル

finrando Finland

フ ィ ン ラ ン ド

oranda Holland

オ ラ ン ダ

noruwē Norway

ノ ル ウ ェ ー

denmāku Denmark

デ ン マ ー ク

indo India

イ ン ド

tai Thailand

タ イ

honkon Hong Kong

ホ ン コ ン

firipin Philippines

フ ィ リ ピ ン

indoneshia Indonesia

イ ン ド ネ シ ア

marēshia Malaysia

マ レ ー シ ア

shingapōru Singapore

シ ン ガ ポ ー ル

myanmā Myanmar

ミ ャ ン マ ー

mekishiko Mexico

メ キ シ コ

burajiru Brazil

ブ ラ ジ ル

aruzenchin Argentina

ア ル ゼ ン チ ン

chiri Chile

チ リ

ejiputo Egypt

エ ジ プ ト

mosukuwa Moscow

モ ス ク ワ

nyūyōku New York

ニ ュ ー ヨ ー ク

rondon London

ロ ン ド ン

pari Paris

パ リ

sōru Seoul

ソ ウ ル

Reading and Writing Practice

I.   Circle the item that does not belong in each group. Check your answers on page 95.

Group A	Group B	Group C	Group D	Group E
アジア	タイ	フィリピン	チリ	インド
ヨーロッパ	ポルトガル	スペイン	ブラジル	ロンドン
アフリカ	ギリシャ	インドネシア	アルゼンチン	ソウル
メキシコ	オランダ	シンガポール	エジプト	ニューヨーク

II.   Listen to audio track 39. Write the words you hear in katakana. Answers are on page 95.

1. _____   6. _____

2. _____   7. _____

3. _____   8. _____

4. _____   9. _____

5. _____   10. _____

III.   Fill in the blanks. Check your answers on page 95.

Country					
City	ニューヨーク	ロンドン	モスクワ	ローマ	パリ

IV.   Listen to audio track 40 and write in katakana the things mentioned and their locations. Check your answers on page 95.

1. _____

2. _____

3. _____

4. _____

5. _____

V.   Which countries and cities listed on pages 70–72 have you been to? Which ones do you want to visit in the future? Make two lists in katakana.

Social Trends and Issues

kūru japan Cool Japan

クールジャパン

abenomikusu Abenomics

アベノミクス

eko eco

エコ

sasutenabiritī sustainability

サステナビリティー

risaikuru recycle

リサイクル

gomi garbage; trash

ゴミ

purasuchikku plastic

プラスチック

petto botoru PET bottle

ペットボトル

bin glass bottle

ビン

kan can

カン

risutora restructuring

リストラ

sekuhara sexual harassment

セクハラ

morahara moral harassment

モ ラ ハ ラ

pawahara power harassment

パ ワ ハ ラ

matahara maternity harassment

マ タ ハ ラ

arafō around 40 years old

ア ラ フ ォ ー

arasā around 30 years old

ア ラ サ ー

kurēmu claim; complaint

ク レ ー ム

toraburu trouble

ト ラ ブ ル

daietto diet

ダ イ エ ッ ト

wākingu pua working poor

ワ ー キ ン グ プ ア

shinguru mazā single mother

シ ン グ ル マ ザ ー

furītā person with no fixed job

フ リ ー タ ー

heito supīchi hate speech

ヘ イ ト ス ピ ー チ

feiku fake

フ ェ イ ク

baisekushuaru bisexual

バイセクシュアル

toransujendā transgender; transsexual

トランスジェンダー

gei gay

ゲイ

rezubian lesbian

レズビアン

kamingu auto coming out

カミングアウト

aidoru idol

アイドル

otaku geek

オタク

kosupure cosplay

コスプレ

shinia senior

シニア

baria furī barrier-free

バリアフリー

kēsu manējā case manager

ケースマネージャー

gyanburu gamble

ギャンブル

doraggu drugs

ドラッグ

Reading and Writing Practice

I.   Circle the item that does not belong in each group. Check your answers on page 95.

Group A	Group B	Group C	Group D	Group E
アイドル	モラハラ	シングルマザー	バリアフリー	ゴミ
オタク	セクハラ	インターン	アラサー	ペットボトル
シニア	リサイクル	レズビアン	リサイクル	ガラス
トラブル	マタハラ	カミングアウト	サステナビリティー	カン
ゲイ	パワハラ	フリーター	エコ	ストレス

II. Listen to audio track 42. Write the words you hear in katakana. Answers are on page 95.

1. _____   6. _____

2. _____   7. _____

3. _____   8. _____

4. _____   9. _____

5. _____   10. _____

III. Listen to audio track 43 and find out what issue (*mondai*) is mentioned in each sentence. Write the answers in katakana. Check your answers on page 95.

1. _____   6. _____

2. _____   7. _____

3. _____   8. _____

4. _____   9. _____

5. _____   10. _____

IV. Which of the social issues mentioned on pages 74–76 are you most concerned about? Make a list.

Hobbies

supōtsu sport

| ス | ポ | ー | ツ | | | | | | | | | | | | | | | | |

saikuringu cycling

| サ | イ | ク | リ | ン | グ | | | | | | | | | | |

kyanpu camping

| キ | ャ | ン | プ | | | | | | | | | | | | | | | | |

haikingu hiking

| ハ | イ | キ | ン | グ | | | | | | | | | | | |

yoga yoga

| ヨ | ガ | | | | | | | | | | | | | | | | | | |

dansu dance

| ダ | ン | ス | | | | | | | | | | | | | | | | | |

sakkā soccer

| サ | ッ | カ | ー | | | | | | | | | | | | | | | | |

tenisu tennis

| テ | ニ | ス | | | | | | | | | | | | | | | | | |

amefuto American football

| ア | メ | フ | ト | | | | | | | | | | | | | | | | |

ragubī rugby

| ラ | グ | ビ | ー | | | | | | | | | | | | | | | | |

sukī skiing

| ス | キ | ー | | | | | | | | | | | | | |

sukēto skating

| ス | ケ | ー | ト | | | | | | | | | | | | | | | | |

marason marathon

マラソン

jogingu jogging

ジョギング

sunō bōdo snowboarding

スノーボード

gorufu golf

ゴルフ

raibu live music concert

ライブ

kurashikku classical

クラシック

rokku rock

ロック

myūjikku music

ミュージック

gitā guitar

ギター

netto sāfin Internet surfing

ネットサーフィン

ī supōtsu e-sport

イースポーツ

sumaho gēmu smartphone game

スマホゲーム

mario Mario

マリオ

pokemon Pokemon

ポ　ケ　モ　ン

anime anime

ア　ニ　メ

manga comics

マ　ン　ガ

karaoke karaoke

カ　ラ　オ　ケ

pachinko pachinko

パ　チ　ン　コ

terebi TV

テ　レ　ビ

dorama drama

ド　ラ　マ

nyūsu news

ニ　ュ　ー　ス

waidoshō variety talk show

ワ　イ　ド　シ　ョ　ー

komedī comedy

コ　メ　デ　ィ　ー

misuterī mystery

ミ　ス　テ　リ　ー

horā horror

ホ　ラ　ー

besutoserā bestseller

ベ　ス　ト　セ　ラ　ー

Reading and Writing Practice

I.   Circle the item that does not belong in each group. Check your answers on page 96.

Group A	Group B	Group C	Group D	Group E
マリオゲーム	ミュージック	ベストセラー	インスタ	スノーボード
マラソン	カラオケ	スキー	コスプレ	ラグビー
スマホゲーム	コンサート	ハイキング	ユーチューブ	ヨガ
イースポーツ	ライブ	ゴルフ	フェイスブック	サッカー
ネットサーフィン	アメフト	キャンプ	ツイッター	マンガ

II.   Listen to audio track 45. Write the words you hear in katakana. Answers are on page 96.

1. _____   6. _____

2. _____   7. _____

3. _____   8. _____

4. _____   9. _____

5. _____   10. _____

III. Listen to audio track 46 and write in katakana the hobbies (*shumi*) each person has. Check your answers on page 96.

1. _____

2. _____

3. _____

4. _____

5. _____

IV.   Which hobbies in the list on pages 78–80 have you practiced? Which ones would you like to try? Make two lists, in katakana.

Who's Who

🎧 Track 47

toyota Toyota

ト	ヨ	タ				

honda Honda

ホ	ン	ダ				

nissan Nissan

ニ	ッ	サ	ン			

kawasaki Kawasaki

カ	ワ	サ	キ			

naiki Nike

ナ	イ	キ				

adidasu Adidas

ア	ディ	ダ	ス		

yamaha Yamaha

ヤ	マ	ハ				

seikō Seiko

セ	イ	コ	ー			

sonī Sony

ソ	ニ	ー				

panasonikku Panasonic

パ	ナ	ソ	ニ	ッ	ク	

rikō Ricoh

リ	コ	ー				

kuroneko yamato Yamato Transport

ク	ロ	ネ	コ	ヤ	マ	ト	

sapporo Sapporo

サッポロ

santorī Suntory

サントリー

asahi Asahi

アサヒ

yunikuro Uniqlo

ユニクロ

kikkōman Kikkoman

キッコーマン

kyūpī Kewpie

キューピー

biru geitsu Bill Gates

ビル・ゲイツ

stību jobuzu Steve Jobs

スティーブ・ジョブズ

baraku obama Barack Obama

バラク・オバマ

donarudo toranpu Donald Trump

ドナルド・トランプ

hirarī kurinton Hillary Clinton

ヒラリー・クリントン

angera merukeru Angela Merkel

アンゲラ・メルケル

mazā teresa Mother Teresa

マザー・テレサ

furīda kāro Frida Kahlo

フ リ ー ダ ・ カ ー ロ

pikaso Picasso

ピ カ ソ

runoāru Renoir

ル ノ ア ー ル

gohho van Gogh

ゴ ッ ホ

dabinchi da Vinci

ダ ビ ン チ

mōtsaruto Mozart

モ ー ツ ァ ル ト

bētōben Beethoven

ベ ー ト ー ベ ン

bītoruzu The Beatles

ビ ー ト ル ズ

madonna Madonna

マ ド ン ナ

biyonse Beyonce

ビ ヨ ン セ

redī gaga Lady Gaga

レ デ ィ ー ・ ガ ガ

meriru sutorīpu Meryl Streep

メ リ ル ・ ス ト リ ー プ

harison fōdo Harrison Ford

ハ リ ソ ン ・ フ ォ ー ド

Reading and Writing Practice

I.   Circle the item that does not belong in each group. Check your answers on page 96.

Group A	Group B	Group C	Group D	Group E
マドンナ	ローソン	ルノアール	パナソニック	ナイキ
メルケル	アディダス	ダビンチ	ユニクロ	トヨタ
クリントン	イオン	ゴッホ	セイコー	カワサキ
オバマ	ビックカメラ	バッハ	ソニー	ニッサン
トランプ	アマゾン	ピカソ	レディー・ガガ	ホンダ

II.   Listen to audio track 48. Write the words you hear in katakana. Answers are on page 96.

1. _____   5. _____

2. _____   6. _____

3. _____   7. _____

4. _____   8. _____

III. Listen to audio track 49 and write the name of the person or company the book is about (*ni tsuite*) in katakana. Check your answers on page 96.

Example: ほんはスティーブ・ジョブズについてです。
         Hon wa sutību jobuzu ni tsuite desu. The book is about Steve Jobs.
Answer: スティーブ・ジョブズ

1. _____

2. _____

3. _____

4. _____

5. _____

IV. Which famous people listed on pages 83–84 do you admire? Make a list in katakana.

V.   Write your full name in katakana. Check it with a Japanese native speaker or at a "your name in Japanese" site on the Internet.

Japanese-English Expressions 🎧 Track 50

eko kā   ecological car

| エ | コ | カ | ー | | | | | | | | | | | | | | | | |

mōningu kōru wake-up call

| モ | ー | ニ | ン | グ | コ | ー | ル | | | | | | | | |

mōningu sābisu breakfast special

| モ | ー | ニ | ン | グ | サ | ー | ビ | ス | | | | | | | | | | | |

furonto   front desk

| フ | ロ | ン | ト | | | | | | | | | | | | | | | | |

tsū shotto   picture of two people

| ツ | ー | シ | ョ | ッ | ト | | | | | | | | | | |

raburabu   lovey-dovey

| ラ | ブ | ラ | ブ | | | | | | | | | | | | | | | | |

kanningu   cheating

| カ | ン | ニ | ン | グ | | | | | | | | | | | |

hai bijon   high-definition television

| ハ | イ | ビ | ジ | ョ | ン | | | | | | | | | | |

afutā kea   after-sales service

| ア | フ | タ | ー | ケ | ア | | | | | | | | | | |

beddo taun   suburb

| ベ | ッ | ド | タ | ウ | ン | | | | | | | | | | |

jetto kōsutā   roller coaster

| ジ | ェ | ッ | ト | コ | ー | ス | タ | ー | | | | | | | |

magu kappu   mug

| マ | グ | カ | ッ | プ | | | | | | | | | | | |

hai tacchi high five

ハイタッチ

donmai don't worry; never mind

ドンマイ

gattsu pōzu victory pose

ガッツポーズ

sukin shippu physical contact

スキンシップ

jīpan jeans

ジーパン

wanpīsu dress

ワンピース

nōsurību sleeveless

ノースリーブ

waishatsu dress shirt

ワイシャツ

furī saizu one-size-fits-all

フリーサイズ

shāpu penshiru mechanical pencil

シャープペンシル

sain pen felt-tip pen

サインペン

majikku marker; felt-tip pen

マジック

hochikisu stapler

ホチキス

maipēsu one's own pace

マ イ ペ ー ス

wan patān always the same

ワ ン パ タ ー ン

sumāto slender

ス マ ー ト

raibu hausu club with live show

ラ イ ブ ハ ウ ス

daiya train schedule

ダ イ ヤ

nō meiku no make-up

ノ ー メ イ ク

gādoman security guard

ガ ー ド マ ン

chiagāru cheer girl (cheerleader)

チ ア ガ ー ル

konsento electrical outlet

コ ン セ ン ト

non arukōru alcohol free

ノ ン ア ル コ ー ル

furī daiaru toll-free number

フ リ ー ダ イ ア ル

bebī kā baby stroller

ベ ビ ー カ ー

man-tsū-man one-to-one

マ ン ツ ー マ ン

Reading and Writing Practice

I.   Circle the item that does not belong in each group. Check your answers on page 96.

Group A	Group B	Group C	Group D	Group E
ワンピース	チアガール	ホチキス	ライブ	ノーメイク
スキンシップ	シングルマザー	マジック	ギター	フロント
ノースリーブ	ガードマン	シャープペンシル	マグカップ	モーニングコール
ワイシャツ	オタク	サインペン	クラシック	シングルルーム
ジーパン	ベビーカー	エコカー	ロック	チェックイン

II. Listen to audio track 51 and write in katakana the thing the speaker is looking for. Check your answers on page 96.

Example: ライブハウス、どこですか。

Raibu hausu, doko desu ka? Where is the club (with live music show)?

Answer: ライブハウス

1. _____

2. _____

3. _____

4. _____

5. _____

6. _____

7. _____

8. _____

9. _____

10. _____

III. Listen to audio track 52 and write in katakana the item or person mentioned in each sentence and the word that describes them. Check your answers on page 96.

Example: あのインターン、マイペースですねえ。

Ano intān, maipēsu desu nē. That intern goes at her own pace, doesn't she?

Answer: インターン、マイペース

1. _____

2. _____

3. _____

4. _____

5. _____

6. _____

7. _____

8. _____

Onomatopoeia and Mimetic Expressions 🎧 Track 53

onomatope onomatopoeia

オ ノ マ ト ペ

mechamecha chaotic, messy

メ チ ャ メ チ ャ

girigiri near the limit; barely

ギ リ ギ リ

mechakucha mess

メ チ ャ ク チ ャ

guchagucha mixed up; mess

グ チ ャ グ チ ャ

gochagocha mixed; mess

ゴ チ ャ ゴ チ ャ

barabara apart; not united

バ ラ バ ラ

chiguhagu incoherent

チ グ ハ グ

garagara empty

ガ ラ ガ ラ

gayagaya noisily

ガ ヤ ガ ヤ

kachikachi rigid; frozen

カ チ カ チ

kankan angry; clang

カ ン カ ン

garigari bony; skinny; rasping

ガ リ ガ リ

The following expressions are often followed by **suru/shimasu** (to do) and used as verbs.

pekopeko behave in a servile manner; hungry

ペ	コ	ペ	コ				

utouto drowse

ウ	ト	ウ	ト				

kuyokuyo worry

ク	ヨ	ク	ヨ				

nikoniko smile

ニ	コ	ニ	コ				

niyaniya smirk

ニ	ヤ	ニ	ヤ				

gorogoro rolling around; doing nothing

ゴ	ロ	ゴ	ロ				

burabura aimless

ブ	ラ	ブ	ラ				

piripiri touchy, easily irritated

ピ	リ	ピ	リ				

bikubiku fearful

ビ	ク	ビ	ク				

kosokoso secretly, behind one's back

コ	ソ	コ	ソ				

kyorokyoro looking around; looking restlessly

キ	ョ	ロ	キ	ョ	ロ	

iraira irritated

イ	ラ	イ	ラ				

dokidoki excited; heart-beating

ド	キ	ド	キ				

Reading and Writing Practice

I. Listen to audio track 54 and write in katakana the thing mentioned and the onomatopoeic word that describes it. Check your answers on page 96.

1. _____

2. _____

3. _____

4. _____

5. _____

6. _____

7. _____

8. _____

9. _____

10. _____

II. Choosing one of the onomatopoeic expressions that goes with the verb します (**shimasu**), describe how you would feel or what you would do in the following situations. Compare your answers with the sample answers on page 96.

1. You are about to take a job interview. _____

2. A neighbor's dog keeps barking. _____

3. You plan to relax at home this weekend. _____

4. You feel sleepy after a big lunch. _____

5. You've got rid of clutter you didn't need. _____

III. Describe your state of mind today using onomatopoeic words.

Answer Key

Page 45, ex I:
Group A アイスクリーム； Group B ケーキ； Group C ケチャップ； Group D ビーフ； Group E ワイン

Page 45, ex II Audio Script:
1. チーズトースト
2. チキン
3. ツナサンド
4. ジュース
5. ミックスピザ
6. シーフードパスタ
7. アイスラテ
8. チョコレートケーキ
9. ストロベリースムージー
10. ビーフカレー

Page 45, ex III Audio Script (answers underlined):
1. たなかさんは<u>シーフードパスタ</u>と<u>ミネラルウォーター</u>ですね。
2. さとうさんは<u>ツナサンド</u>と<u>ストロベリースムージー</u>ですね。
3. なかむらさんは<u>ハンバーガー</u>と<u>フライドポテト</u>と<u>コーラ</u>ですね。
4. ありささんは<u>チャーハン</u>と<u>ギョーザ</u>と<u>アイスコーヒー</u>ですね。
5. なおみさんは<u>ランチセット</u>ですね。

Page 49, ex I:
Group A ビール； Group B パーク； Group C ジュース； Group D コーヒー； Group E ドーナツ

Page 49, ex II Audio Script:
1. コンビニ
2. スターバックス
3. レストラン
4. エレベーター
5. ガソリンスタンド
6. ファミレス
7. マクドナルド
8. パルコ
9. コミュニティーセンター
10. ショッピングモール

Page 49, ex III Audio Script:
1. メリーさんは、デパートにいきました。
2. エミリーさんは、スポーツクラブにいきましたよ。
3. いとうさんは、コミュニティーセンターにいきました。
4. テレサさんは、コインランドリーにいきました。
5. メイメイさんは、イオンのカフェにいきました。
6. モティさんは、ショッピングモールのマクドナルドにいきました。

Page 53, ex I:
Group A ヒーター；Group B タオル；Group C コーヒーカップ；Group D ティッシュ；Group E シャンプー

Page 53, ex II Audio Script:
1. ダイニング
2. キッチン
3. ドア
4. ベランダ
5. トイレットペーパー
6. カーペット
7. シーツ
8. テレビ
9. エアコン
10. ティッシュ

Page 53, ex III:
1. ベッド
2. バスルーム
3. リビング
4. キッチン
5. リビング

Page 53, ex IV Audio Script (answers underlined):
<u>ダイニングテーブル</u>とリビングの<u>カーペット</u>と<u>クッション</u>、それからベッドルームの<u>カーテン</u>と<u>スタンド</u>、それから、<u>シーツ</u>と<u>タオル</u>と<u>スリッパ</u>もいるわね。

Page 57, ex I:
Group A カーテン； Group B セキュリティー； Group C グレープ； Group D パスワード；
Group E プライバシー

Page 57, ex II Audio Script:

1. スマホ
2. コピペ
3. グーグル
4. ログイン パスワード
5. コミュニケーション

6. セキュリティー ソフト
7. ユーザー
8. オンライン
9. ホームページ
10. テクノロジー

Page 57, ex III:

Possible Answers

Social Media:	フェイスブック	ツイッター	インスタ
Digital Device:	スマホ	ケータイ	タブレット パソコン
US Hi-Tech Company:	グーグル	アップル	

Page 57, ex IV Audio Script:

1. もんだいは、アクセスです。
2. もんだいは、パスワードです。
3. もんだいは、ログインです。

4. もんだいは、ダウンロードです。
5. もんだいは、ソフトです。

Page 61, ex. I:

Group A バスツアー；　Group B フライト；　Group C トラベル；　Group D メール；　Group E バイク

Page 61, ex II Audio Script:

1. モノレール
2. ガイドブック
3. ビジターセンター
4. オンライン　チェックイン
5. ルームサービス

6. パスポート
7. シャトルバス
8. バイキング
9. コインロッカー
10. チケットカウンター

Page 61, ex III Audio Script (answers underlined):

1. デパートまでバスでいきます。
2. ゲートまで、エレベーターでいきます。
3. バスターミナルまで、シャトルバスでいきます。
4. ビジターセンターまでタクシーでいきます。
5. ペンションまでレンタカーでいきます。

Page 65, ex I:

Group A Mサイズ；　Group B クレジットカード；　Group C レシート；　Group D ユーロ；　Group E ホテル

Page 65, ex II Audio Script:

1. ドル
2. クレジットカード
3. アマゾン
4. ネットショッピング
5. ディスカウントショップ

6. サービスカウンター
7. セルフレジ
8. サイズ
9. キャッシュ
10. ファッション

Page 65, ex. III Audio Script (answers underlined)

1. ギフトは、デパートでかいました。
2. メガネは、ネットショップでかいました。
3. パソコンは、ビックカメラでかいました。
4. ワインは、デューティーフリーでかいました。
5. バスツアーのチケットはコンビニでかいました。

Page 69, ex I:

Group A フレックスタイム；　Group B ライバル；　Group C オフレコ；　Group D グローバル；　Group E バイヤー

Page 69, ex II Audio Script:
1. グローバルビジネス
2. サラリーマン
3. スケジュール
4. イノベーション
5. プロジェクトリーダー
6. ステークホルダー
7. フィードバック
8. コーポレートガバナンス
9. サプライチェーン
10. チームワーク

Page 69, ex III Audio Script:
1. マーケティングは？
2. ミーティングは？
3. クライアントのオフィスは？
4. ライバルは？
5. フィードバックは？
6. インターンのレジュメは？
7. ベンチャーのプレゼンは？
8. チームリーダーは？
9. プロジェクトのスケジュールは？
10. ロジスティクスは？

Page 73, ex I:
Group A メキシコ；　Group B タイ；　Group C スペイン；　Group D エジプト；　Group E インド

Page 73, ex II Audio Script:
1. イギリス
2. ホンコン
3. ニューヨーク
4. ドイツ
5. ブラジル
6. フィリピン
7. メキシコ
8. パリ
9. シンガポール
10. ヨーロッパ

Page 73, ex III: アメリカ；　イギリス；　ロシア；　イタリア：　フランス

Page 73, ex IV Audio Script (answers underlined):
1. オフィスは、アメリカです。
2. ミーティングは、シンガポールのホテルです。
3. クライアントは、ヨーロッパです。
4. プレゼンは、ソウルです。
5. ビジネスチャンスは、アジアとアフリカです。

Page 77, ex I:
Group A トラブル；　Group B リサイクル；　Group C カミングアウト；　Group D アラサー；
Group E ストレス

Page 77, ex II Audio Script:
1. リサイクル
2. ビン
3. セクハラ
4. アベノミクス
5. ヘイトスピーチ
6. アイドル
7. ペットボトル
8. シングルマザー
9. ダイエット
10. アラフォー

Page 77, ex III Audio Script:
1. もんだいは、プラスチックのリサイクルです。
2. もんだいは、ネットのヘイトスピーチです。
3. もんだいは、ドラッグです。
4. もんだいは、フェイクニュースです。
5. もんだいは、シニアのネットギャンブルです。
6. もんだいは、インターンのセクハラやモラハラです。
7. もんだいは、アベノミクスのリスクです。
8. もんだいは、ワーキングプアです。
9. もんだいは、バリアフリーのトイレです。
10. もんだいは、シンガポールのオフィスのリストラです。

Page 81, ex I:
Group A マラソン；　Group B アメフト；　Group C ベストセラー；　Group D コスプレ；　Group E マンガ

Page 81, ex II Audio Script:
1. スポーツ
2. カラオケ
3. ヨガ
4. スマホゲーム
5. クラシックミュージック
6. アメフト
7. テレビドラマ
8. キャンプ
9. パチンコ
10. ニュース

Page 81, ex III Audio Script
1. しゅみは、テニスとサッカーです。
2. しゅみは、スノーボードとスキーです。
3. しゅみは、マンガとアニメです。
4. しゅみは、ダンスとキャンプです。
5. しゅみは、カラオケとヨガです。

Page 85, ex I:
Group A マドンナ　Group B アディダス；　Group C バッハ；　Group D レディー・ガガ；　Group E ナイキ

Page 85, ex II Audio Script:
1. サッポロ
2. ユニクロ
3. ビル・ゲイツ
4. ルノアール
5. ビートルズ
6. ベートーベン
7. クロネコヤマト
8. バラク・オバマ

Page 85, ex III Audio Script:
1. ほんは、スティーブ・ジョブズについてです。
2. ほんは、ナイキとアディダスについてです。
3. ほんは、モーツァルトについてです。
4. ほんは、オバマとクリントンについてです。
5. ほんは、フリーダ・カーロについてです。

Page 89, ex I:
Group A スキンシップ；　Group B ベビーカー；　Group C エコカー　Group D マグカップ；
Group E ノーメイク

Page 89, ex II Audio Script:
1. ライブハウス、どこですか。
2. コンセント、どこですか。
3. フロント、どこですか。
4. ワイシャツ、どこですか。
5. ホチキス、どこですか。
6. ベビーカー、どこですか。
7. サインペン、どこですか。
8. ガードマン、どこですか。
9. マグカップ、どこですか。
10. ジェットコースター、どこですか。

Page 89, ex III Audio Script:
1. あのインターン、マイペースですねえ。
2. あのモーニングサービス、ベストですねえ。
3. あのチアガール、スマートですねえ。
4. あのビール、ノンアルコールですねえ。
5. あのプロジェクト、マンツーマンですねえ。
6. あのツーショット、セクハラですねえ。
7. あのシャツ、フリーサイズですねえ。
8. あのライブハウス、バリアフリーですねえ。

Page 92, ex I Audio Script:
1. カスタマーは、カンカンです。
2. スケジュールは、メチャメチャです。
3. あのレストランは、ガラガラです。
4. あのカップルは、サバサバしています。
5. あのパンは、フワフワしています。
6. このクッキーは、サクサクですねえ。
7. クライアントはイライラしています。
8. オフィスは、ゴチャゴチャしています。
9. インターンは、クヨクヨしています。
10. グループは、バラバラです。

Page 92, ex II:
1. ドキドキ
2. イライラ
3. ゴロゴロ
4. ウトウト
5. サバサバ